THE POCKET

Aussie English

Published in 2024
by Gemini Adult Books Ltd
Part of Gemini Books Group

Based in Woodbridge and London
Marine House, Tide Mill Way
Woodbridge, Suffolk IP12 1AP
United Kingdom

www.geminibooks.com

Text and Design © 2024 Gemini Books Group
Part of the Gemini Pockets series

Cover image: Greenscreen FX/Shutterstock (hat); Macrovector/Freepik
(kangaroo)

ISBN 978-1-78675-174-4

A CIP catalogue record for this book is available from the British Library.

Printed in China

10 9 8 7 6 5 4 3 2 1

MIX
Paper | Supporting
responsible forestry
FSC® C008047

THE
POCKET

Aussie
English

G:

Contents

Introduction

Although the DNA of the world's inhabitants is 99 per cent the same, it's the 1 per cent difference where things get interesting. So, although the UK and Australia share the same alphabet, their vocabularies are another matter.

We all know the King's English is proper-like, infused with reserve and good manners. It is punctuated and well-rounded. Its sentences contain all they must, in correct order. But, in the land down under, everything is upside down. Words are cut down to size, meanings given the Liverpool kiss and grammar is optional.

Think of this book as your secret weapon. Unlocking the mysteries of a place where bathrooms are without carpet, temperatures below 18°C considered winter, and deadly spiders in your boot no cause for alarm. To lessen the culture shock and have you fitting in like a snag on the barbie, read on.

Discover that depending which country you're standing in, thongs can be either flip-flops or underwear, rubbers are erasers or condoms, and a trunk is either a car boot or travel luggage.

You'll learn that an offie is a bottle-o, a laptop is a lappy and a tea break is a smoke-o. You'll be able to distinguish between pissing down and a piss-up, and before you know it, you'll be sitting down with a pot – or a middie or schooner – in a rubbedy, and getting on with the locals like a house on fire, rather than drinking with the flies.

This book can save you a whole lot of trouble!

AUSSIE

—

ENGLISH

AUSSIE	ENGLISH
ABC	Australian Broadcasting Corporation
Aboriginal (*adj.*)	First Nations peoples of Australia
Accadacca	Australian band AC/DC
agro, also **aggro**	aggressive
ANZAC	Australian and New Zealand Army Corps
Anzacs	soldiers of the Australian and New Zealand Army Corps
ankle-biter	child
arvo	afternoon
ASIO (pronounced AZIO)	Australian Security and Intelligence Organisation
Aussie	an Australian
Aussie rules	Australian rules football (AFL)

AUSSIE	ENGLISH
avo	avocado
award rate	minimum rate of pay

apple islander

native or resident of Tasmania

The first apple trees in Tasmania were planted on Bruny Island by Captain Bligh in 1788. By the late 1800s Tasmania was one of the world's biggest producers. Tasmanian apples were being exported all over the world and the island became synonymous with its famous product.

B

AUSSIE	ENGLISH
baby boomers	older Australians, born between 1946 and 1964
back of beyond	middle of nowhere
back of Bourke	back of beyond
backyard	back garden
bail	to cancel plans/leave hurriedly
banana bender	Queenslander
barbie	barbecue
beaut(y)	great, marvellous
beef road	cattle trains moving livestock from the outback
bell (give someone a)	call someone on the phone
bikkie	biscuit
billabong	pond or a pool of water

AUSSIE	ENGLISH
billy	can or tin for boiling water
bindi eye, bindy	prickle from a low-lying weed
bitch-face	facial expression of disdain
block (of land)	plot (of land)
blowfly, blowy	a very large fly
bludger	a lazy person
bluebottle	a type of jellyfish with a nasty sting
bluey	redhead
boardies	swimming shorts
bogan	redneck
bonza	great/good
boomerang	Indigenous Australian hunting weapon/article to be returned

B

AUSSIE	ENGLISH
booze bus	police vehicle used to catch drunk drivers
bottle-o	off-licence
bowser	petrol pump
brekky	breakfast
Bris-vegas	Brisbane
brolly	umbrella
brumby	wild horse
bubbles	champagne, or similar (prosecco, crémant, cava, etc.)
Buckley's chance	no chance
buck's night, buck's party	stag night
budgie smugglers	speedos or swim briefs
buggered	exhausted, tired

AUSSIE	ENGLISH
bull dust	bullshit, fine dust found in the outback
bungalow	single-storey holiday cottage
bunyip	Indigenous Australian mythical creature
bush	the countryside/outback
bush, go	take off to the countryside
bushfly	fly (smaller than a blowfly)
bushed	tired
bushman, bushy	a person who knows the land and the outback
bushranger	highwayman
bush tolly	campfire
byo	bring your own, usually alcohol

AUSSIE	ENGLISH
cack	laugh
cactus	dead/broken
Captain Cook	have a look around
cardboardeaux	box wine
cark it	die
carry on	lark about
centre	central Australia
check, to pass in one's	die
chips (potato)	crisps
chock-a-block	full to capacity
choppers	false teeth
Chrissie	Christmas
chunder	vomit
clacka	bum
clapped out	worthless

coat hanger, the

Sydney Harbour Bridge

Built in 1932, using almost 53 tonnes of steel, and 134 metres above the water, the Sydney Harbour Bridge remains the tallest steel arch bridge in the world.

AUSSIE	ENGLISH
cobber	friend, mate
cocky	farmer
cold one	a beer
come good	turn out all right
comfort station	toilet
compo	compensation
contraceptive	condom/Durex
cordial	fruit squash
cossie	swimsuit
cove	chap
crack the shits	get angry at someone or something
cracker	great
crayon	coloured pencil
creek	non-perennial stream
crook	ill/sick/out of order

AUSSIE	ENGLISH
Cross, The	Kings Cross, nightclub area of Sydney
crow eater	South Australian

cuppa

cup of tea

Alfred Bushell opened Australia's first tea shop in 1883 in what is today Queensland. Sixteen years later, Bushell's sons established Bushell's Company in Sydney.

AUSSIE	ENGLISH
dag	sheep's wool matted with turd/term of endearment or mild abuse
daks	trousers
dam	pond/reservoir
damper	bread without yeast cooked in ashes of camp fire
dead ringer for	spitting image of
dead set	telling the truth
deli	food shop
digger	Australian soldier
dill	idiot
dingo	Australian wild dog
dirt road	unsurfaced road
dob someone in	drop someone in it
dodgy	suspect

didgeridoo

Indigenous Australian musical instrument

The original didgeridoos, played in the north of Australia 40,000 years ago, were made from fallen eucalyptus branches that had been hollowed out by termites. The instrument has one underlying tone and a series of overtones, altered by the player's lips.

D E

AUSSIE	ENGLISH
dog's eye	pie
donga	penis
draft	conscription
drapes	curtains
drongo	idiot
drunk	full
dry, the	dry season in the tropics
duco	paintwork on cars
duds	best clothes
durry	cigarette
eggplant	aubergine
esky	portable icebox/cooler

dunny

toilet

A dunny was originally an outside toilet, which would be emptied, in towns and cities, by the dunny man with his dunny cart. Now used to mean any toilet, the word derives from the British word 'dunnekin', meaning 'earth closet', formed from the two words, 'dung' and 'ken', meaning 'house'.

F

AUSSIE	ENGLISH
fair dinkum	genuine/excellent
fanny	female pubic area
fibro	asbestos board
financial	paid up/solvent/in the black
fiver	five dollars (AUD)
flake	shark meat
flash flood	sudden river overflow
footy	generic term for rugby union, rugby league, Australian rules or soccer
fossick	have a look around
freeway	motorway
full, smashed, maggoted, blind, shitfaced, hammered	drunk

furphy

absurd or improbable story

Around the time of the First World War, Furphy Foundry water tanks were used by Australian diggers (soldiers). The often unlikely tales told around these tanks, as they were moved from place to place, became known as 'furphies'.

G

AUSSIE	ENGLISH
galah	parrot/idiot
galvo	galvanized iron
gander	look closely
garbo	dustman
g'day	good morning/afternoon/evening
get off my back	leave me alone
give someone heaps	wind someone up
globe	light bulb
goanna	a very large lizard
good oil	inside information
good on ya	well done/good for you
googie egg	boiled egg
goon	box wine
gravel road	untarred road

AUSSIE	ENGLISH
grazier	farmer (on land he owns himself)
grog	alcohol
grouse	great
gumboots	Wellingtons
gum tree	eucalyptus tree

guernsey

sports jersey/shirt (often sleeveless)

A typical Australian rules shirt is sleeveless, though a guernsey may sometimes have long sleeves. To 'get a guernsey' means to be selected for a team.

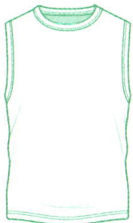

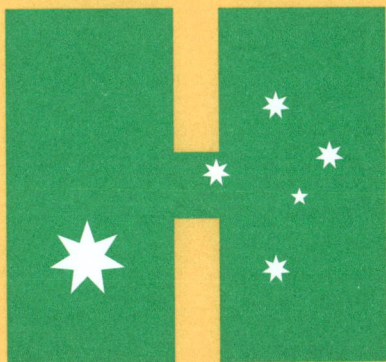

AUSSIE	ENGLISH
hang eleven	male surfing nude
hang ten	ten toes over the nose of the surfboard
hard yakka	hard work
hook	to steal
hoo-roo	cheerio/goodbye
hotel	pub
hot-water service	immersion heater
howyagoin?	How are you?
humpy	shanty
icy pole, also ice block	ice lolly
incorporated (company)	public limited company
Indigenous Australian	Aboriginal, First Nations peoples of Australia
intersection, road	junction
interstate	to or from another state

Huey

the god of surf

It is said that in the outback during times of drought, struggling farmers would appeal to the 'God of the Rains', saying, 'Send it down, Hughie' ('Huie' and 'Hewie' are other variants). By 1981, surfers had adopted Huey as their own god, with their appeal for waves: 'Send 'em up, Huey.'

J K

AUSSIE	ENGLISH
jacked (off)	fed up with
jackeroo	male pupil on cattle/sheep station
jillaroo	female pupil on cattle/sheep station
Joe Blake	snake
jumbuck	sheep
kero/kerosene	paraffin
kick in	contribute money
king wave	enormous/irregular wave
Kiwi	New Zealander
knock	deride/criticize

joey

young kangaroo

The first recorded use of joey was in 1839. Some believe it is derived from an Indigenous Australian word *joè*, but its origin is uncertain. It is now used to refer to any young animal or even a young child.

L

AUSSIE	ENGLISH
lairy	gaudy/flashily clothed
lamb's fry	lamb's liver
lappy	laptop
lay-by	put a deposit on an article in a shop
leg over	procreate
leg-up	head start
lippy	lipstick
lollies	sweets
lounge	three-piece suite
lounge room	lounge/living/sitting room
lurk	scheme/trick for achieving one's ends

larrikin

hooligan/ruffian

An unruly or violent young man. Alternatively,
a mischievous or boisterous person, irreverent
and with a disregard for convention. The word
is thought to be derived from the word 'lark',
as in 'larking about'.

AUSSIE	ENGLISH
Macca's	McDonald's
Manchester	household linen
masonite	hardboard
mate	friend/buddy
metho	methylated spirits/meths
MHR	Member of the House of Representatives (Federal)
middie, also **middy**	drinking measure (285 ml, or half a pint)
milk bar	dairy and general grocery shop
misery guts	gloomy person
missus	wife
mob	flock of sheep/crowd of people
mozzie	mosquito
muffler (of a car)	silencer

mulga

hardy outback plant

Mulga is a drought-resistant, indigenous acacia found throughout inland Australia. Its branches funnel water down to its unusually long taproot and its needle-like leaves covered with fine, silver-grey hairs also help it to survive in arid regions for up to 50 years. Spikes of bright yellow flowers generally bloom between March and October, after heavy rain.

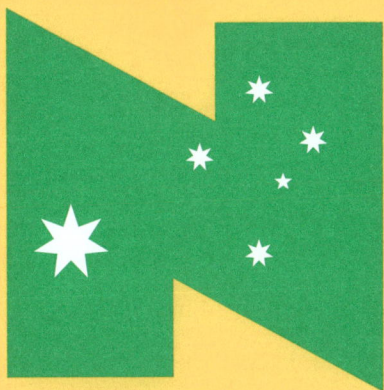

AUSSIE	ENGLISH
nature strip	grass verge
never-never	remote outback
Noah's ark	shark
no-hoper	ne'er-do-well
nosh-up	big meal
no standing (road sign)	no waiting
no worries	that's all right/no problem
no wuckas	a truly Aussie way to say 'no worries'
nuddy	naked

AUSSIE	ENGLISH
odometer	trip meter
offsider	mate/assistant
oi	hey
old fella	penis
oldies	parents
outback	remote Australia
oval	sports field
overlander	cattle drover
overseas	abroad
Oz	Australia

P

AUSSIE	ENGLISH
paddock	field
parka	anorak
parmi	chicken parmigiana
pav	pavlova

pash

to kiss passionately

'Pash' as an abbreviation of 'passion' has been around in Britain since the late nineteenth century, but 'pash' meaning 'passionate kiss' emerged in Australia in the 1960s, as did 'pash session' for 'passionate kissing and/or heavy petting'.

AUSSIE	ENGLISH
pick (*v.*)	spot/identify
pissed	drunk
pissing down	raining hard
piss-up	booze-up
play possum	pretend to be asleep/dead/ ignorant
pom/pommy	English person
pony	drink measure
postie	postman
pot	medium-sized glass of beer
prang	bump/accident (with cars)
premier	head of an Australian state
prime minister	Australian federal prime minister
public holiday	bank holiday
public service	civil service

R

AUSSIE	ENGLISH
rack off	the less offensive way to tell someone to fuck off
ranga	redhead
rapt	keen on something/someone
ratbag	rascal
rego	car registration
restroom	public toilet
ringer	stockman
rip	dangerous ocean current
ripper	fantastic
road train	long-distance lorry with several trailers
rockmelon	cantaloupe melon
roo	kangaroo

AUSSIE	ENGLISH
root rat	someone who enjoys sex (maybe a little too much)
rover	field position in Australian rules football
rubbedy	pub (derived from 'rub-a-dub-dub')
rubbish (*v.*)	put down
rubbish tin	waste-paper basket
ruckman	field position in Australian rules football
rugged-up	wrapped up against the cold
run (for election)	stand (for election)
runners (shoes)	trainers
rust bucket	old car

AUSSIE	ENGLISH
saltbush	bush found in arid areas
salvo	member of Salvation Army
sand groper	a West Australian
sandshoes	plimsolls/gym shoes
sanger	sandwich

schooner

a large glass of beer

Australia has names for various sizes of beer glass. A small glass is a 'pony'; a half-pint is a 'middy' or 'middie'; and a 'schooner' is nearly a full pint (425 ml in all states other than South Australia, where it is 285 ml).

AUSSIE	ENGLISH
scone (off one's)	head (off one's)
sealed (road)	tarmac-surfaced road
sea wasp	lethal jellyfish
sedan	saloon car
semi-trailer	articulated lorry
servo	petrol station
shallots	spring onions
shandy	a half-and-half mix of beer and lemonade
shark bait	swimmer furthest from the shore
shark biscuit	young children swimming in the sea
sheila	girl/woman
shooting through (like a Bondi tram)	to leave in a hurry

AUSSIE	ENGLISH
shout (*v.* and *n.*)	to buy a round of drinks
sickie	day off work when sick (or not)
singlet	vest
skite	boast
skiter	boaster
skivvy	polo-neck top
slab	a carton of beers
slack	lazy
sleepout	extension to a house, enclosed verandah
sling (*n.*)	underhand commission
sling off (*v.*)	deride/slag off
sly grogging	illicit drinking
smoke-o	tea break
smokes	fags/cigarettes

AUSSIE	ENGLISH
snags	sausages
snaky	irritable/touchy/angry
spag bol	spaghetti bolognaise
spinifex	desert grass
sport	mate/pal/old man
squatter (early settlement period)	person who occupied and fenced open land
squirrel grip	a tackle applying pressure to the testicles
station	a large sheep or cattle farm
station wagon/wagon	estate car
sticky tape	Sellotape
stinger	lethal jellyfish
stock route	track for droving cattle
stockyard	cattle pen
stoked	really happy

S'traya

Australia

In addition to 'S'traya', Australia is also known as Oz and Down Under. The word Australia derives from the Latin *australis*, and dates back to second-century legends of a mythical 'unknown southern land' – *Terra Australis Incognita*. From 1804, Australia began to replace New Holland, the name given by Dutch seafarer Abel Tasman in 1643. Indigenous Australian names for the land include *Uthuru* in the Midwest, *Barna* in the Murchison region and *Kurrek* in the Wemba Wemba language of Victoria.

AUSSIE	ENGLISH
stretcher	camp bed
strides	trousers
Strine	Australian slang
stroller	pushchair/pram
stubbies	a pair of shorts
stubby	a short, squat beer bottle
stuffed	really tired
sunbake	sunbathe
sundowner	happy hour
supper	late evening snack
surfies	surfers
swag	bundle of belongings/ sleeping gear
Sydneysider	Sydney resident

T

AUSSIE	ENGLISH
tank (in the bush)	water storage in dry areas
Tassie	Tasmania
taxi-truck	van-hire service
teller (in a bank)	cashier
Territorian	inhabitant of the Northern Territory
thingo	thing/thingummy
thongs	flip-flops
tinkle	give someone a call on the phone
tinny	can of beer/runabout
tits up	failed
tow-truck	breakdown vehicle
tracky daks	sweatpants (tracksuit pants)
Track, The	Alice Springs–Darwin road

AUSSIE	ENGLISH
tradie	tradesperson
truck (*n.*)	lorry
truck (*v.*)	transport by lorry
tube	can of beer
tucker	food
turd	poop

two-up

traditional gambling game

Often played on Anzac Day, a 'spinner' throws two pennies into the air and players bet on whether the coins will both fall heads up, both tails up or with one head and one tail, a Ewan.

AUSSIE	ENGLISH
underground mutton	rabbit (as a food)
undies	underpants

ute/utility vehicle

single-cab truck

A 'ute', or 'utility vehicle', is a small truck with a two-door cab. Ford Australia coined the term when they launched their Coupe Utility in the 1930s. 'Utes' are seen as an integral part of Australian culture; even the use of the American term 'truck' is viewed as unpatriotic.

AUSSIE	ENGLISH
vest	waistcoat/sleeveless knitted pullover

vintage (n.)

a mature wine

At the cheaper end, based on *vin blanc*, Australian soldiers used 'point blank', 'von blink' and 'plinkety-plonk', subsequently widely adopted as 'plonk'.

AUSSIE	ENGLISH
wait on	wait for

walkabout

*long walk of unknown duration
or goal to get away from it all*

An Indigenous Australian term for returning temporarily to traditional ways of being, Bruce Chatwin described going walkabout as 'a ritual journey', while M. G. Godwinsdatter has described a walkabout as a 'time of reflection of the soul, a return to one's roots and family ancestry … a time of balance to harmonize with the sounds and sights of the great land of Australia'. The word is also used simply to describe a period of, perhaps unexplained, absence.

AUSSIE	ENGLISH
wanker	jerk, literally 'masturbator'
wet, the	the rainy season in the tropics
wharfie	docker
willy-willy	cyclone/tropical dust storm
winery	vineyard
within cooee of	in shouting distance
woolgrower	sheep farmer
woomera (Indigenous Australian)	spear-launching device
woop-woop	middle of nowhere, somewhere very far away
wowser	spoil-sport/puritan
yeah, nah	yes, I heard you, but no
yobbo	hooligan
zucchini	courgette

ENGLISH

–

AUSSIE

ENGLISH	AUSSIE
aboriginal (*adj.*)	First Nations peoples of Australia, Indigenous Australian
abroad	overseas
absurd or improbable story	furphy
AC/DC (rock group)	Accadacca
afternoon	arvo
aggressive	agro, also aggro
alcohol	grog
Alice Springs–Darwin road	The Track
angry	hot under the collar, blow a fuse, spit the dummy, cranky, do your 'nana
anorak	parka
articulated lorry	semi-trailer
asbestos board	fibro
Australia	Oz, S'traya
Australian (*n.*)	Aussie
Australian and New Zealand Army Corps	ANZAC
Australian Broadcasting Corporation	ABC

Australian rules football (AFL)	Aussie rules, aerial ping-pong
Australian Security and Intelligence Organisation	ASIO (pronounced AZIO)
Australian slang	Strine
Australian soldier	digger
Australian wild dog	dingo
avocado	avo

B

ENGLISH	AUSSIE
back garden	backyard
bank holiday	public holiday
barbecue	barbie
beer, a	a cold one
beer bottle, short, squat	stubby
beer, can of	tube, tinny
beer, large glass of	schooner
beer/lemonade mix	shandy
beer, mid-size	middie, or middy
beer, small glass of	pony
beers, a carton of	slab
best clothes	duds

big meal	nosh-up
biscuit	bikkie
boast/boaster	skite/skiter
boiled egg	googie egg
booze-up	piss-up
box wine	goon, cardboardeaux
bread without yeast cooked in ashes of camp fire	damper
breakdown vehicle	tow-truck
breakfast	brekky
bring your own (usually alcohol)	byo
Brisbane	Bris-vegas
bullshit	bull dust
bum	clacka
bump/accident (with cars)	prang, stack, bingle
bundle of belongings/ sleeping gear	swag
bush found in arid areas	saltbush
buy a round of drinks	shout (*v.* and *n.*)

ENGLISH	AUSSIE
call someone (on the phone)	bell, tinkle (give someone a)
cancel plans/leave hurriedly	bail
can or tin for boiling water	billy
cantaloupe melon	rockmelon
car registration	rego
cashier (in a bank)	teller
cattle drover	overlander
cattle trains (moving livestock from the outback)	beef road
central Australia	centre
champagne	bubbles
chap	cove
cheerio	hoo-roo
chicken	chook
chicken parmigiana	parmi
child	ankle-biter
Christmas	Chrissie
cigarette	durry
civil service compensation	public service compo

condom/Durex	contraceptive
conscription	draft
contribute money	kick in
cooked chicken	dead chook
countryperson	bushwhacker
countryside/outback	bush
courgette	zucchini
crayon	coloured pencil
crisps	chips (potato)
cup of tea	cuppa
curtains	drapes
cyclone/tropical dust storm	willy-willy

D

ENGLISH	AUSSIE
dairy and general grocery shop	milk bar
dangerous ocean current	rip
day off work (sick or not)	sickie
dead/broken	cactus
deride/criticize/slag off	knock, sling off

desert grass	spinifex
die	cark it, pass in one's check
disdainful expression	bitch-face
docker	wharfie
drinking (illicit)	sly grogging
drop someone in it	dob someone in
drunk	full, smashed, maggoted, blind, shitfaced, hammered
dry season in the tropics	the dry
dustman	garbo

E

ENGLISH	AUSSIE
eggplant	aubergine
English person	pom/pommy
enormous/irregular wave	king wave
estate car	station wagon/wagon
eucalyptus tree	gum tree
exhausted	buggered
extension to a house, enclosed verandah	sleepout

F

ENGLISH	AUSSIE
fags/cigarettes	smokes
failed	tits up
false teeth	choppers
fantastic	ripper
farmer	cocky
farmer (on land the farmer owns)	grazier
fed up with	jacked (off)
female pubic area	fanny
female pupil on cattle/ sheep station	jillaroo
field	paddock
field position in Australian rules football	rover
fine dust found in the outback	bull dust
First Nations peoples of Australia	Indigenous Australians
five dollars	fiver
flip-flops	thongs
flock of sheep/ crowd of people	mob

English	Aussie
fly (smaller than blowfly)	bushfly
fly (very large)	blowfly, blowy
food	tucker
food shop	deli
friend	mate, cobber
fruit squash	cordial
fuck off (reasonably polite)	rack off
full to capacity	chock-a-block

G

ENGLISH	AUSSIE
galvanized iron	galvo
gambling game	two-up
gaudy/flashily clothed	lairy
genuine	fair dinkum
get a place in the team	get a guernsey
getting angry at someone or something	cracking the shits
girl/woman	sheila
gloomy person	misery guts

god of surf	Huey
good morning/afternoon/ evening	g'day
grass verge	nature strip
great/good	grouse, cracker, bonza

H

ENGLISH	AUSSIE
half-pint (of beer)	pot
happy hour	sundowner
hard work	hard yakka
hardy outback plant	mulga
head	scone
head of an Australian state	premier
head start	leg-up
hey	oi
highwayman	bushranger
hooligan	yobbo
hooligan/ruffian	larrikin
How are you?	howyagoin?
hunting weapon (Indigenous Australian)/ article to be returned	boomerang

ENGLISH	AUSSIE
ice lolly	icy pole, ice block
idiot	dill, drongo, galah
ill/sick/out of order	crook
immersion heater	hot-water service
in shouting distance	within cooee of
inhabitant of the Northern Territory	Territorian
inside information	good oil
irritable/touchy/angry	snaky

ENGLISH	AUSSIE
jellyfish (lethal)	sea wasp
jellyfish (with a nasty sting)	bluebottle
jerk	wanker
junction	intersection (road)
just a minute	wait on

K

ENGLISH	AUSSIE
kangaroo	roo
kangaroo, young	joey
keen on something/ someone	rapt
kids at the beach	shark biscuits
kiss (*v.*)	pash

L

ENGLISH	AUSSIE
lamb's liver	lamb's fry
laptop	lappy
lark about	carry on
late evening snack	supper
laugh	cack
lazy	slack
lazy person	bludger

leave in a hurry	shoot through (like a Bondi tram)
leave me alone	get off my back
lengthy walk to get away from it all	walkabout
light bulb	globe
lipstick	lippy
lizard (very large)	goanna
long-distance lorry with several trailers	road train
long way away, a	back of Bourke
look around	Captain Cook, have a fossick
look closely	gander
lorry	truck (*n.*)
lounge/living/sitting room	lounge room

ENGLISH	AUSSIE
male pupil on cattle/ sheep station	jackeroo
male surfing nude	hang eleven

Manchester	household linen
masonite	hardboard
mate/assistant	offsider
mate/pal/old man	sport
McDonald's	Macca's
Member of the House of Representatives (Federal)	MHR
methylated spirits/meths	metho
middle of nowhere	back of beyond, woop-woop
minimum rate of pay	award rate
mosquito	mozzie
motorway	freeway
musical instrument made from a hollow bough (Indigenous Australian)	didgeridoo
mythical creature (Indigenous Australian)	bunyip

ENGLISH	AUSSIE
naked	nuddy
native or resident of Tasmania	apple islander
ne'er-do-well	no-hoper
New Zealander	Kiwi
nightclub area of Sydney (Kings Cross)	The Cross
no chance	Buckley's chance
no waiting	no standing (road sign)
no worries	no wuckas

ENGLISH	AUSSIE
off-licence	bottle-o
old car	rust bucket
older Australian (born between 1946 and 1964)	baby boomer

P Q

ENGLISH	AUSSIE
paid up/solvent/in the black	financial
paintwork on cars	duco
paraffin	kero/kerosene
parents	oldies
parrot	galah
pavlova	pav
penis	donga, old fella
person who knows the land and the outback	bushman, bushy
person who occupied and fenced open land (early settlement period)	squatter
petrol pump	bowser
petrol station	servo
pie	dog's eye
plimsolls/gym shoes	sandshoes
plot (of land)	block (of land)
police breath-testing vehicle	booze bus
polo-neck top	skivvy
pond, or a pool of water	billabong

ENGLISH	AUSSIE
pond/reservoir	dam
poop	turd
portable icebox/cooler	esky
postman	postie
pretend to be asleep/ dead/ignorant	play possum
prickle from a low-lying weed	bindi eye, bindy
procreate	leg over
pub	rubbedy
public limited company	incorporated (company)
public toilet	restroom
pushchair, pram	stroller
put a deposit on an article in a shop	lay-by
put down	rubbish (*v.*)
Queenslander	banana bender

R

ENGLISH	AUSSIE
rabbit (as a food)	underground mutton
raining hard	pissing down

rainy season in tropics	the wet
rascal	ratbag
really happy	stoked
really tired	stuffed
redhead	bluey, ranga
redneck	bogan
remote Australia	outback
remote outback	never-never
road, untarred/unsurfaced	gravel road/dirt road
ruckman	field position in Australian rules football
rugby union, rugby league, Australian rules or soccer (generic term)	footy

ENGLISH	AUSSIE
saloon car	sedan
salvo	member of the Salvation Army
sandwich	sanger
sausages	snags
scheme/trick for achieving one's ends	lurk

Sellotape	sticky tape
sex enthusiast	root rat
shanty	humpy
shark	Noah's ark
shark meat	flake
sheep	jumbuck
sheep farmer	woolgrower
sheep or cattle station, large	station
sheep's wool matted with turd (also a term of endearment or mild abuse)	dag
shorts, pair of	stubbies
silencer (of a car)	muffler
single-storey holiday cottage	bungalow
single-cab truck	ute/utility
snake	Joe Blake
soldiers of the Australian and New Zealand Army Corps	Anzacs
South Australian	crow eater
spaghetti bolognaise	spag bol
spear-launching device	woomera (Indigenous Australian)
speedos or swim briefs	budgie smugglers
spitting image of	dead ringer for

spoil-sport/puritan	wowser
sports field	oval
sports jersey/shirt	guernsey
spot/identify	pick (*v.*)
spring onions	shallots
stag night	buck's night, buck's party
stand (for election)	run (for election)
steal (*v.*)	hook
stinger	lethal jellyfish
stockman	ringer
stock route	track for droving cattle
stockyard	cattle pen
stream, non-perennial	creek
stretcher	camp bed
strides	trousers
sudden river overflow	flash flood
sunbathe	sunbake
surfers	surfies
surfing with ten toes over the front of the surfboard	hang ten
suspect (*adj.*)	dodgy
sweatpants (tracksuit pants)	tracky daks
sweets	lollies
swimming shorts	boardies
swimsuit	cossie

Sydney Harbour Bridge	the coat hanger
Sydney resident	Sydneysider

ENGLISH	AUSSIE
take off to the countryside	go bush
tarmac-surfaced road	sealed road
Tasmania	Tassie
tea break	smoke-o
telling the truth	dead set
that's all right/no problem	no worries
thing/thingummy	thingo
three-piece suite	lounge
tired	bushed
toilet	dunny, comfort station
to or from another state	interstate
tradesperson	tradie
trainers	runners
transport by lorry	truck (*v.*)
trip meter	odometer
trousers	daks
turn out all right	come good

ENGLISH	AUSSIE
umbrella	brolly
underhand commission (*n.*)	sling
underpants	undies

ENGLISH	AUSSIE
van-hire service	taxi-truck
vest	singlet
vineyard	winery
vomit	chunder

WY

ENGLISH	AUSSIE
waistcoat/sleeveless knitted pullover	vest
waste-paper basket	rubbish tin
water storage in dry areas	tank (in the bush)
well done/good for you	good on ya
Wellingtons	gumboots
West Australian	sand groper
wife	missus
wind someone up	give someone heaps
wine, a mature	vintage (*n.*)
worthless	clapped out
wrapped up against the cold	rugged up
yes, I heard you, but no	yeah, nah

wild horse

brumby

As Australia was colonized, horses escaped or were abandoned, and became wild. Historian Eric Rolls suggests that the term 'brumbies' may derive from a Private James Brumby, who abandoned his horses in 1804 when he was transferred from New South Wales to Tasmania. Other suggestions are that the name may derive from an Indigenous Australian language spoken in Queensland or New South Wales; from the Irish *bromaigh*, meaning 'colts'; or from the Barambah Creek in Queensland.

AUSSIE
IDIOMS

AUSSIE	ENGLISH
aerial ping-pong	Australian rules football
all froth and no beer	more talk than action
all over red rover	finished
all the go	popular craze
all your Christmases have come at once	all your dreams have come true
ankle-biter	child
arse about	back to front
as cross as a frog in a sock	exasperated
Australian tai chi	carrying a full tray of beers from the bar, through the crowd, to your table, without spilling any beer
bachelor's handbag	supermarket roast chicken in a plastic bag
bald as a bandicoot	completely without hair
bean-counter	accountant
beat around the bush	not address the issue

AUSSIE	ENGLISH
bee's dick	miniscule distance
better half	partner
big bikkies	large amounts of money
big hat, no cattle	more talk than action
bit of all right	good-looking
Bob's your uncle	there you have it
bottom-of-the-harbour scheme	tax avoidance
boys in blue	police officers
Broken Hill time	half an hour behind everyone else
brown bomber	parking inspector
built like a brick shithouse	solidly muscled
bust your guts	wholehearted effort
busy as a centipede on a hot plate	didn't stop all day

AUSSIE	ENGLISH
cack-handed	left-handed
call a spade a spade	straight talk
carked it/cashed their cheque	died
cheeky little possum	loveable rogue
chuck a u-ey	U-turn (*v.*)
come a gutser	fall over
dingo's breakfast	a scratch and stretch, no food
do a runner	escape without paying what you owe
dog's breakfast	disorganized
don't fret your freckle	relax
don't stick your nose in it	don't interfere
do the bolt	to leave without goodbyes
drier than a pommy's bathmat	very dry indeed

AUSSIE	ENGLISH
drinking with the flies	friendless
drop-kick	fool
drown some worms	go fishing
fair crack	to give a reasonable opportunity
family jewels	testicles
fancy bending the elbow?	would you like a drink?
fat as a butcher's pup	plump
feeling clucky	wanting children
flash as a rat with a gold tooth	showy dresser
flat out like a lizard drinking	busy
flat out like a maggot on a chop	very busy – 'Have I been busy at work? Flat out like a maggot on a chop, mate!'
flogging the plastic	racking up credit-card debt
from arsehole to breakfast	from top to bottom

AUSSIE	ENGLISH
frothing at the mouth	annoyed
fugly	frightfully ugly
full as a boot	very drunk
full of beans	lively
get it down ya	eat/drink this
get off at Redfern	coitus interruptus
get on like a house on fire	immediate friendship
getting on it	clear focus on imbibing alcohol
get up my goat	irritate me
given the arse	sacked
give someone a bell	to phone someone
glue on the shoe	slow horse/dog/human
go down the gurgler	business failure
go like hot cakes	successful sales
got more balls than Keno	brash, overconfident

AUSSIE	ENGLISH
grew another leg	good performance
hasn't got a bean	empty wallet
hasn't got a hope	no chance
hasn't got two bob to rub together	without cash, not even coins
have a great face for radio	ugly
have tickets on yourself	pompous
have to run around in the shower to get wet	thin person – 'Sharon's stopped eating Tim Tams. She's lost so much weight she has to run around in the shower to get wet!'
having a bad trot	a run of bad luck
hip-pocket nerve	wallet
hit the road	time to leave
horizontal folk dancing	sexual intercourse
hotter than a shearer's armpit	very hot

AUSSIE IDIOMS

AUSSIE	ENGLISH
hot under the collar	fiery temper
I could eat a horse and chase its rider	experiencing low blood sugar
I could eat a horse if you took its shoes off	I'm starving
I'm drier than a drover's dog	I need a drink
I'm strapped	I have no money
in a lather	fearful
I need to throw on the nose bag	I'm ready to eat
let one rip	pass wind
like a rat up a drainpipe	rapidly
like flies round the dunny door	a large crowd
little Aussie battler	average Joe
loose unit	risk-taker

AUSSIE	ENGLISH
mad as a cut snake	vicious
man is not a camel	I am thirsty
men in grey suits	sharks
more than you can poke a stick at	huge numbers
not in a month of Sundays	event unlikely to happen no matter how long is given
not much chop	no good
not my cup of tea	something does not sit well with me
not the full quid, not playing with the full deck, the lift doesn't go to the top floor, only has one oar in the water	not very intelligent
off his chops	blind drunk
off the beaten track	remote areas
off the rails	losing track
off with the fairies	daydreamer

make a galah of yourself

behave foolishly

The galah is an abundant, widespread and predominantly pink Australian cockatoo. Their name derives from the Indigenous Australian Yuwaalaraay-language word *gilaa*. This use of galah may derive either from the look of the birds or what are seen as their silly antics.

AUSSIE	ENGLISH
off your trolley	rendered nonsensical by alcohol
off your tucker	unwell
old fossil	senior citizen
on a good wicket	beneficial situation
on a sticky wicket	tricky situation
on the ball	intelligent
on the blink	out of order
on the knocker	perfect summation
on the nose	suspicious
on the outer	unpopular
on the swipes	searching dating apps for love
on the turps	heavy drinker
on the wagon	not drinking
on the wrong track	imminent failure

AUSSIE IDIOMS

AUSSIE	ENGLISH
paper shuffler	administrator
pay through the nose	high price
pull your socks up	do better
put it on the never-never	request for credit
put your head down	work harder
ridgey-didge	on the level, trustworthy
right as rain	agreement
rough end of the pineapple	worse side of the bargain
run around like a chook with your head cut off	busy, but ineffective
run out of legs	get tired
run rings around	be better than
runs on the board	good reputation
scarce as hens' teeth	unlikely to be found despite looking
seven-course meal	meat pie and six-pack of beer

AUSSIE	ENGLISH
she'll be apples	everything will work out
she'll be right	hopeful of good outcome
sick as a dog	hungover, flu, an upset stomach
six of one, half a dozen of the other	both solutions are the same
skin and blister	sister
skinny as a rake	painfully thin
so wet it would bog a duck in boots	very wet indeed
spanner monkey	car mechanic
sparrow's breakfast	very small crumb, insufficient
spit the dummy	have a babyish outburst
stone the crows	I don't believe it
tackle applying pressure to the testicles	squirrel grip
take a squizz	worth further attention

AUSSIE	ENGLISH
taken to the cleaners	to lose everything
that'll buff right out	major damage to vehicle
the green room	ocean
the old man	father
the scenic route	lost
throw the toys out of the pram	have an angry blow-off
to be dudded	sold something inauthentic
to be fleeced	cheated
to carry on like a pork chop	to behave stupidly
to cop it sweet	take something on the chin without complaining
to piss in someone's pocket	to flatter someone
to take a punt on something	to take a risk
to take a shine to	to like someone

AUSSIE	ENGLISH
two-pot screamer	an inexperienced drinker
up the duff	pregnant
up your bum	a drinking toast
useless as a chocolate teapot	unworkable
useless as a glass door on a dunny (toilet)	impractical
wearing one's birthday suit	naked
wearing the wobbly boot	very inebriated
were you born in a tent?	a reminder to close the door
what do you do for a crust?	how do you earn your living?
what's the damage?	how much?
whip-round	gather money for someone in need
wrap your laughing gear around this	an invitation to eat or imbibe

AUSSIE	ENGLISH
write your own ticket	a bet with so little chance the bookmaker lets you set the odds
your blood's worth bottling	an expression of admiration
you scrub up nicely	a compliment to someone on looking good
you wouldn't be dead for quids	life is wonderful
you wouldn't take them fishing	boring company

PICTURE CREDITS